THE CURIOSITIES

The Curiosities

CHRISTOPHER REID

FABER & FABER

First published in 2015
by Faber & Faber Ltd
Bloomsbury House
74–77 Great Russell Street
London WC1B 3DA

Typeset by Hamish Ironside
Printed by Martins the Printers, Berwick-upon-Tweed

A CIP record for this book is available from the British Library

ISBN 978–0–571–32145–2

2 4 6 8 10 9 5 3 1

The Contents

To Róisín

THE CURIOSITIES

The Clowns

Who is whose clown, precisely?
His Majesty *El Rey de Jamón*
demands to know. Rebellion and laughter
are rife at court, his witty *bufón*
loses no opportunity for mockery or sport
at his expense, and he himself is too slow
to mount a defence against digs and sideswipes
that keep coming. What's so funny?
His courtiers are no help – he hasn't any;
ditto, the palace guard; so he's on his own
and finding it hard to keep a straight face.
Is it time for him to resign his crown
and put on motley? He turns to the mirror:
¡Coño! It's happened already . . .

The Cat

There was no letting about it: no cautious
loosening of drawstrings, no tipping up
and shaking out. The cat stepped forth
of its own accord. With a yawn
that had a snarl in it, and an absent-minded
hoisting of its tail, already it looked bored
with the fact of its own existence.
So? What else was new?
The disdain, the brusqueness, the lack of tact
of your typical, blunt-headed tom:
all present and correct!
Just time to allow its arched and writhing
back to be stroked, an attempt at tenderness
acknowledged with a petulant squawk,
and the next minute it had left by the window –
away, I dare say, to some other
pressing errand of unsubtle innuendo.

The Chocolate

In the following pages, I propose to articulate
a comprehensive erotics of chocolate.
Other scholars have gone some way to illuminate
aspects of the matter; Buscott and Strumpf
on commodity and fetishisation,
and Yoshimura on *jouissance*
have been particularly helpful;
but the complicity of the chocolate itself,
its secret desire to yield both form and essence
to the darkness and blood-heat of the mouth,
entering and becoming one
with the eater, has not until this moment
been sufficiently taken into account.
Naturally, I expect my argument
to meet certain objections,
and I shall confront these in my opening chapters.
But first, why don't you close your eyes,
part your lips, and let me pop a square
that's already starting to melt between my fingers,
on to your moist and acquiescent tongue?

The Cry

The child woke to a cry not his.
It came from beyond: a cry
of the absolute night. But it wasn't
a beast. It wasn't a ghost.
It wasn't a truck or a train. It was
a closer cry, of something like pain,
deep-fetched, both pushing and dragging,
torn, with its long-straggling, humanoid roots
protesting, from a soil that clogged and clung
and was reluctant to let it be born,
breathe air, take flight.
Perhaps some, even most, of the cry
agreed, with a lullaby croon
or wheedle, preferring to sleep,
or to die. But the rest of the cry
had put up a fight against itself:
an urgent, delirious skirmish.
Which it must win. Which it did,
with a short-lasting whimper
of triumph and release.
In the peace that followed,
the child lay awake, unable to explain
why he was stirred by a thing
so ugly, so sad and so frightening;
nor why he wanted to hear it again.

The Coin

Being dead, I was ready for
the journey. They put a coin,
one obol, the standard fare,
under my tongue – now still,
but not yet cold.
I had not been told
that this would happen.
But a shut mouth is, I thought,
as safe a purse as any.
The taste, which would have made me
wince and scowl before,
and spit the nasty thing out,
was neither here nor there.
So I took my pill without a fuss,
and set off like a child
walking for the first time
to catch the morning bus,
under a sky both bright
and hazy, fraught
with promise of adventure.
The world was just beginning,
there could be no end,
and the coin was my sole
possession, my secret friend.
So long as my lips kept tight,
what could go wrong?
Oh, I wish they had warned me
about the boatman who
with his strong, hard fingers –

stinking of fish, or something –
prised my jaw open and withdrew
the mite, the token,
the less than a button,
that he claimed as his due.

The Calabash

Having fashioned the first man out of sticks and mud,
God looked at him and thought, 'Not bad.' But Man
was of a different opinion.
Equipped from the outset with the twin gifts
of speech and dissatisfaction, Man said,
'God, be honest, are you really happy
with this bodge, this shoddy bricolage,
this job at best half done?' 'What do you mean?'
God asked. 'I need a mate,' Man told him,
'and I need one fast.' God was flustered;
he'd run out of ideas already; so he replied,
'If you're so certain what you want,
tell me how to make it.' Glancing about,
Man's eye fell on a plump gourd hanging from a tree:
a calabash. 'That will do,' he said.
God nodded and set to work, adding
legs, arms and a head to the lovely roundness,
with other details that would make Woman a match
for the stick-and-mud figure who stood by, watching.
When he had finished, God rubbed his hands, delighted.
But Man was less sure, remembering the pure shape
that had first caught his fancy: both virginal and gravid,
suspended improbably from that scruffy tree.
'Take it or leave it,' God said. Man remained
undecided, and Woman, too, had her proliferating doubts.

The Cloud

When the precocious Tadworth twins, Nigel and Phil,
drew me aside in the changing room to explain
how things really worked, what men did to women,
the body parts involved and the manner in which they
    were used,
it was as if a great, blanking cloud had lifted
and a new one taken its place.

The Children

Four or five perhaps,
she's imitating her mother
as she crouches to secure a grip
under the armpits of her brother,
who hasn't yet learned to walk
and sits puppyish on his haunches.
An experimental and risky
but passively accepted hoick
launches him to her height,
where, after a moment's
non-calamitous sway,
he's held tight in a hug
that looks like unqualified love.
His stubby arms stick out
stiff as a crucifixion;
his lower body's as slack
as a deposition from the cross;
from this new, calmly enjoyed
eminence he can survey
both the world of sorrow and loss
and his sister's beautiful hair.
Yet he doesn't seem to mind
when her embrace breaks
and she lets him slither back down,
a suddenly unmanageable sack.

The Colt

Tearaway, tomboy,
with your bones still growing
and your hair still flowing,
pay no attention to us
as you canter and keep cantering
with lovely, lively indolence
and no fuss or fears
in the seemingly unbounded
paddock of your years.

The Chill

after Petrarch

Diana's lover could not have been more thrilled,
when, through a piece of luck, he caught an eyeful of her
skinny-dipping in a chilly pool,
than I was by the strapping highland shepherd girl
stopped there to wash the strip of cloth that keeps
her wild blond hair from being blown about –
with such effect that, even under a fiery sky,
I shivered all over with a lascivious chill.

The Chisel

after Baratynsky

Eyes boring into the block,
the sculptor can make out
a nymph at its centre,
so that his veins catch fire
and his heart goes pounding in pursuit.
For all his desire, however,
he is still wholly attentive to his art:
peck by peck, and in no evident hurry,
his chisel begins the finicky task
of exposing the bashful goddess.
Hours, days, years fly past
in this humdrum business; and yet
the last veil will not have been stripped
from the object of his prowess
until, registering his feelings
through the chisel's foreplay,
Galatea herself
quickens with desire, her gaze
meets his and she carries
the great genius away
to a convulsive bliss.

The Café

Newspaper-readers
outside at the sunny café:
a becalmed regatta.
Tall, indolent palm trees
topped with shuttlecock feathers.
Breast-pocket balconies
up to roof level
on three sides of the square:
stage-set for an operetta, viewed from the sea.
In the middle, a fountain,
too grand to have been turned on.
Yelps and clatter
of shop-blinds raised
for mid-morning trade.
Motor traffic
snarling and tooting elsewhere.
I watch you tear
your breakfast croissant,
then dress its fresh wound with butter.
The mouth I devoured
with kisses last night
has private business right now,
as does my own.
That's you, this is me.
A flake of pastry has strayed
to your upper lip.
My coffee tastes pleasantly bitter.

The Cherry

Tell me, why should the first cherry,
the first cherry of summer,
always be the best?
Not the first bag,
though that may be good,
but the first piece of fruit.
Selected for its flawless shine,
tugged from its stalk,
introduced between tongue and palate
to be weighed there briefly,
assayed chiefly
for plumpness and firmness,
before committal to the teeth,
after less than a second
of poised, of poignant,
refusal to betray its secret,
it succumbs to a single bite
that broaches the taut skin,
releasing a sharp-sweet spurt,
and mouth and cherry
rush to combine their juices
in a joyous union
that cannot be repeated
for four full seasons.
Why not? Finding out –
or, rather, attempting to –
accounts for many a bellyache
and much heaviness of heart.
Forget reasons, just take

that first, ritual
taste-burst as it comes,
and, when you've sucked the stone clean,
leave the rest
of the bag you've just bought,
leave all the rest
of summer's abundant cherry crop
well alone.

The Catapult

'Please, have a proper look,'
the assistant said. He took the carving
in both hands, appraised it.
Rudimentary female figure,
in a fair wood he couldn't name.
Bare, forked. Expression: aloof,
contained. Arms sketched in relief,
the standard ballerina pose.
A W for breasts. And then
the parted legs, ending in,
not feet, but sort of knobs,
to which, presumably, the tough,
projectile-twanging leather –
whatever – lost now, could be tied.
Between the legs: smooth wood.
That's where the hunter's thumb
must have rested. He wanted
to touch, too, but couldn't –
not with the assistant waiting
for him to decide.
'I'll have to think about it,'
he said, and gave it back.
'No problem,' she replied.

The Critics

First night, and the critics are in,
in force. They have seen this piece
before, of course – more often than they
can remember. Notepads in laps
and preconceptions ready,
they have taken up their prime
positions around the bed. For them,
it has to be right first time.
They do not care that this is unrehearsed,
and no amount of special pleading –
lack of script, inexperience,
the wrong conditions – will excuse
stage fright or a botched performance.
The actors enter, the woman backwards,
but leading the man
in an unsteady, inch-by-inch,
smooching and grappling dance,
till, as if tripped, they tilt
and tip over, still in a clinch,
him on top, stage-centre.

The Collarbone

Lady, I don't know you,
but I know your collarbone
really quite well.
All night, as the party
has marshalled and mingled us
through these rooms,
I have kept it in view.
It's a spellbinding thing,
as you must be aware,
having chosen precisely
that cut of dress
to frame and enhance
its loveliness, that fine
gold chain to show,
with its wandering line,
how proudly it sweeps,
how steeply the shadowed
hollows behind it plunge.
If I asked you nicely . . .?
No: I shall never put
my lips, my nose,
my tongue there to taste
the tart/sweet perfume
you no doubt touched in
left/right at the start
of the evening. Too bad.
Yet I am glad enough
to be privy to a sight
so rare: the contour

of your superb collarbone,
fluid in the flicker and flare
of party candlelight.

The Cougar

Of all the celebrated beauties of her day,
she was the most exotic and conspicuous.
The 'fur coat and no knickers'
of the powerfully slouching beast,
a cougar, that she led on a leash
whenever she went shopping, excited
speculation of the obvious sort;
and yet her intimate friends
reported she was chaste, piously
inclined, devoted to charitable works
and kind to the sick and dying.
Still, the paparazzi, vying to get
the best and closest shots they could –
or dared, with such a supple, watchful,
speed-packed, fang-flashing pet
to be wary of – cared nothing for that.
What they and the world saw
was the classic scary couple:
glamorous woman and killer cat –
image answering to some delinquent need
of the masculine mind.

The Clearing

Was it Biba, or was it the schmatta bazaar
of Carnaby Street?
Did a narcoleptic sitar muddle the air
like incense,
or was there some more laddish beat?
The Stones? The Doors?
Had somebody pinned the Pirate Jesus face
of Che Guevara to the wall, or Waterhouse's
orgasmically grieving, teenaged Lady of Shalott?
No matter. What I do recall
is a clearing in the jungle, where, on a table,
half a dozen shallow potpourri bowls,
brimming with petal-coloured knickers,
encircled the bellied bulk
of an old, contemplative cash register.
Oblation? Prayer? Or what?
Please don't ask me to explain, or to remember
anything else. I was there.

The Costume

Fourteen, and the perfect casting for Viola,
though we weren't to know it till he put on the costume.
Bigby-Squires, remember? Later head of school,
then Balliol – rugger blue, a first in Greats –
went on to a smirchless career in the Foreign Office:
gongs, knighthood, the lot. Frankly, his speaking of the
  lines
wasn't so hot, but, as soon as he tripped on in that full,
pinch-waisted brocade dress and dinner-plate ruff –
which seemed to offer his pout up for a kiss –
we were in thrall. Both *coup de théâtre* and *coup de*
  foudre!
Becoming Sebastian, he lost much of his glamour,
though I can attest there were not a few in the hall
whose heads remained disarrayed by the double-take.
For some the effect lingered on: certain sixth-formers
flouting custom to address him by his first name,
and that ex-army gym instructor who, according to
  rumour,
broke down over Christmas and failed to return to his
  post.
The only record is a photo of the curtain call,
which shows the costume as a thing of dazzlement,
while Viola himself – so to speak – is a blur, a ghost.

The Courtesan

after Rilke

The sun of Venice
will refine my hair
to gold: all alchemy's
glorious outcome.
My brows are like
her bridges: look
how they arch the silence
and menace of my eyes,
which have entered into
a secret alliance
with her canals,
so the sea itself
surges, ebbs
and throbs in them.
Whoever's seen me
once at once
resents my lap-dog,
with which, in fits
of absent-mindedness,
my hand, which no heat
has ever touched
but which is invulnerable
and bejewelled,
will toy. And boys,
the scions of ancient houses,
perish from my kisses,
as if poisoned.

The Canes

Suddenly, there was a craze for canes
among the junior masters.
Mr Warburton had one; Mr Peckwood; Mr Soames,
   of course.
One week, we gambolled under their pastoral
   stewardship;
the next, police-state caprice and brute force
ran the show. You could be pounced on and thrashed
for seemingly nothing at all. No one explained
why the rules had changed, or what the new rules were,
but we accepted them like peculiar weather.
Not all the canes were canes as such:
they might be any swishable stick or handy bludgeon
that could descend at speed, smack accurately, and sting.
Another odd thing: they'd christened their weapons
with old-fashioned girls' names – Mildred, Ethel, Doris –
that might have been the names
of their mothers or aunts. A certain ping-pong bat
was known as Gertrude. Funny, that.

The Coward

. . . Orpheus, mind you, they booted out of the
   Underworld,
and without the wife he had come to fetch home.
He wasn't even allowed a glimpse of the real woman,
only her wraith, because, just like a musician,
he evidently lacked the balls for the job and was not
   prepared
to die for love, as Alcestis was. Instead,
he wangled his way down there alive. Which is why
they hit him so hard, setting him up to be killed
by a bevy of women . . .
(And so on and so forth: the sort of stuff,
quibbling and camp, you might hear
any night of the week around the port and nuts,
letting it waft up into the booze-addled air.
The wonder is Plato bothered to write it all down.)

The Couch

Such plot as there is
centres on the couch.
She's the bored housewife,
sitting there, bored.
The doorbell rings, she answers
and he, the pizza delivery boy,
enters. Where else to go
but the couch? Once on board,
it's astounding how quickly
clothes come off and they're
giving each other the works.
Few acting skills
are either required or displayed,
though her hyper capers
offer more to the eye
than his earnest pounding –
as uninspired
as the physical jerks
of an ironing-board.
No wonder the camera's
bent on reducing them
to a trite synecdoche:
piston and pouch.
Meanwhile, it's easy
to overlook the couch,
whose service as bawd
and board, as trysting-place
and marriage-bed,
has been a *sine qua non*.

Veteran of a thousand
identical scenes, it alone
acquits itself
with something like grace:
the eternal supporting player,
dignified, sturdy, self-effacing
and uncredited.

The Celibate

after Ibn Faraj

She would have, but I said no,
defying the devil in my head.
Unveiled, she came to my room,
radiant in the gloom,
and slipped between the sheets.
But I knew I mustn't yield.
Lying beside her all night,
I was like a young camel
muzzled from his mother's teats.
Or a visitor to a garden,
intoxicated by the fragrance,
but forbidden to pick a single flower.
Thank God for willpower!
Imagine the damage, if, like a herd
of buffalo on the rampage,
I had broken into that field.

The Crowbar

Since you enquire, this is the very implement
Father McNulty carried on his night patrols,
ever on the *qui vive* for courting couples,
prising them apart with it if he took the view
matters were getting out of hand.
There's some would tell you it's as well the practice
has been banned, but you'd not believe
the number of souls he saved in that businesslike fashion
from everlasting hellfire.

The Calm

Becalmed, we had little to do
but watch ice grow.
It crept and clenched to form,
horizon-wide, a lid
beneath which whales, our old
companionable foe,
wantonly hid. That white spell
would have gripped
and crushed our vessel
like a walnut shell, had not the captain
sent down men with saws
to hew a dock, a jagged
trench or puddle, where we must wait
and pray. No wind to bear it away,
the stench of blubber thickened,
coating throats and sickening stomachs.
Stiff with grease, my beard
refused the razor. Under that curse
of peace, I took up a sperm tooth
and a sail needle, enthused to try
some scrimshaw work –
Britannia, say, or Amphitrite
side-saddle on a seahorse,
or just my wife in her new crinolines.
Nothing appeared. The tooth lay,
greasy too, athwart my hand.
I pondered it like an obstinate
problem in geometry:
a warped cone, flattened here

and bulging there, defying me
with a beauty of its own;
epitome of laws
I was not yet fit to understand.

The Cacophony

We're eight years old. We're on our feet
and doing sea shanties. Something annoys
our music teacher, Mrs Bryce.
With her mysterious, grown-up powers
of sorrow, bitterness and spite,
she taunts and cows us. 'Stupid boys!
You'll stay here through your break, if need be,
till you've got it right. You'll stay here
till tomorrow!' We lunge into the verse again.
'*In Amsterdam there lived a maid,*' we sing
shrilly and raggedly . . . '*And she was mistress . . .*'
Smiting the keyboard, Mrs Bryce
drives us and the music on. Somehow we reach
the chorus: '*A-roving, a-roving,
for roving's been my ru-i-in*' –
which is where we falter, as always.
Somebody dares to giggle; others join in.
'Stop that at once!' There are tears
in Mrs Bryce's eyes. 'Stop that horrid din!'

The Corbel

The church stands out in farmland,
small but stalwart,
the spare and holy space inside
guarded by corbels,
a ring of them, posted like sentinels
and facing every approach.
Unaccountably weather-enduring
after almost nine hundred years,
these sports of the mason's fancy –
sandstone doodles, curiosities, jokes –
have more to do with magical
fireside tale-telling
than with gospels and epistles.
Human grotesques
and animal improbabilities –
a dog snuggling up to a rabbit –
cock their snook
at reason and decorum.
Forget the weather,
it's a wonder the logical Puritans
left them alone:
especially that most notorious
female imp
shown parting her genitalia,
shockingly large and deep,
and challenging us to contemplate
the holy space inside.

The Caryatids

Sisters, look at us, standing in a row,
holding up a crumbling portico
and crumbling with it. But who are we?
Does anybody know? Nymphs,
or what? We're certainly not
goddesses, not even demi-goddesses,
just nameless drabs and functionaries
balancing on our squashed tresses
a great, smashed lump of architecture
that nobody needs now. Put on parade
several thousand years ago, we've kept
our inner selves a secret, even while
our planes and curves have been
so flagrantly displayed. Our sculptor,
with his hack, academic touch, made us
semi-nude: drapes from the hips down,
nakedness above, with breasts
small and neat enough not to fluster
the most susceptible prude,
and faces so blank you'd never guess
we had our own feelings. But we do;
oh yes, we do. So why don't we break rank?
I fear the equal spaces between us mean
that, while we share our load equally,
we're trapped by it, too: feet on plinths,
heads jammed against ceilings, we're
the precise size, the very measure,
of our own imprisonment and servitude,
and can never aspire to any gesture

of non-compliance. So our defiance
must work more subtly. Aided by time,
by the weather, by our steadfast wills,
we crumble as we stand. Our suffering
is sublime, a slow, stone death,
and we take pride in enduring it together.

The Cochineal

Now that the absolute
freshness of our brides
is less highly valued
than it was before,
the makers and merchants
of cochineal, that costly substance,
of which every fluid ounce
represents the gore
of a thousand crushed insects,
have been the first and loudest
to denounce and deplore
the moral laxness of our times.

The Call

The female passes and the male,
perched high above with other males
constructing their elaborate roost,
emits his characteristic call,
a two-part whistle: first,
brief rising glissando, pause, then
appoggiatura and slide back down
to a slightly lower pitch.
The female hears but does not look up;
in fact, she appears to stiffen
and accelerate her pace. It is far from clear
what advantage, if any, the male has gained
by this display, as mating seldom follows.
One conjecture: that this is a signal
primarily from male to male,
designed to warn of a hostile approach
and, by the suggestion of greater numbers,
to keep the threat at bay.

The Conceit

It is a fals report, that my Lord the Erle of Ickenham
was bannyshed from Covrt, for the immodest
lengthe and girthe, vnwarrantabyll costlinesse
and lewd verysimilitude of his codd-piece.
Nay, rather, he conspired to enflame Her Maiestie's yre,
by the sophisticall expatiating,
before her fayrest and most fauord Ladie-in-Waiting,
on a svchlike (*mutatis mutandis*) womannysh nether
    adornement,
the which he termed, wantonlie, Merkyn, or Mynge, or
    Merrie-thovght.

The Cyborgs

While most of their literature remains
at a primitive stage,
their love poetry shows
remarkable development.
I believe this could prove a Golden Age.
Addressing the pains
and other malfunctions of love,
their lyric poets –
male, female, hermaphrodite –
write with a precision and force
that put to shame
their merely human counterparts.
Beside them, we tend to look
either callow or coarse.
Their superequipped brains, too,
have allowed them to master
the most intricate verse forms,
rivalling the achievements of Languedoc.
I have seen one knock off
a double inverted sestina
faster than you or I would take
to produce a rhyming couplet,
and it contained
both more heartache and more bytes
of sexotechnical information
than all the sonnets of Shakespeare.
Their flights of eloquence
appear unconstrained;
they are young, they are immortal –
and it's early days yet.

The Cowhand

after Theocritus

I was mindin' to give her a little peck,
when Miss Eunice swung right round
and hissed like a rattler:
'Git yer paws off, mister! What,
smooch a mangy cowpoke like you?
Don't think I hold with those hick ways o' yours.
I learned my kissin' in the big city,
no galoot like you 's gonna touch these lips –
no, not in his dreams. Why, take a look at yer:
the way you talk, the way you come on,
yer mouth all tobaccy-stained, yer fingernails filthy –
and you reek to high heaven.
Let me go this minute, or I'll need a long, hot soak!'
At that, she spat in the sawdust three times,
all the while frankly sizin' me up
between simpers, smirks and battin' her eyelashes,
till in the end she broke right out
in a big, scoffin', high-an'-mighty guffaw.
Goldarnit, my blood boilt there and then.
My face turned red with the mortification of it,
red 's a rose in the mornin' dew.
Then she up and left. But it still riles,
a minx like her wouldn't give the time o' day
to a fine buckaroo like me.

The Courier

after an anonymous fourteenth-century Welsh poet

Go, Gogolesque member,
on an errand for your master!
Hop out of my trousers
and take an urgent message
to my darling far from here:
tell her I want her with me.
Be off now – bounce all the way
on your two tireless testicles.
Don't dawdle or droop. Be bold.
Blood-proud, handsomely helmeted,
present yourself like a trooper;
stand staunch as you salute her;
your brisk and dashing manner
should let that fine lady know
where her true interests lie.
If she doubts, drive the point home
with deft thrusts and debonair flourishes:
that kind of argument counts
for more than rank or riches,
so bang on till she cries 'Yes!'
and comes without further ado.

The Courtesies

What a night, and what a neighbourhood,
to be out in – out and up to no good!
Edge-of-town dinge and darkness,
where an intermittent wind
chafes leaves and litter
into a skirmish of dancing
and drives a shaft of ice
straight to the bones of any creature
wild enough to be chancing
such a late hour.
Here's one: frail, farouche,
dressed in a coat she hugs tight
and too little underneath,
pacing on tip-tappy heels
between safety zones of lamplight,
every halt and about-turn
charged with a chemical mix
of wariness and weariness.
Here's another: more shadowed,
more in ambush,
but just as strung, as he waits
either to press his advantage
or to retreat.
It isn't decided yet, and won't be
till certain signals are exchanged,
courtesies so discreet –
such a matter of fine negotiation
between fearful and bold –
it's anyone's guess

whether these two night scavengers
will gain the respite they long for
from the persecuting cold.

The Cottage

Bashful in best suits, the two young men
stood side by side and listened to the charge.
They mounted no defence. The facts were plain
and the law must take its course. The magistrates
conferred briskly, before meting out
the usual reprimand and punishment
and hurrying on to the next case.
But was true justice done? What if Yeats –
or Crazy Jane – were right about the place
that Love had pitched his mansion in?
Smelly and uncomfortable, no doubt,
but nothing at all to do with crime, or wrong, or sin?

The Caterwaul

What to you may be a mere
tomcat caterwaul
is to both singer and serenaded one
music of shape and meaning,
fastidious in its anguish as flamenco,
with which it shares certain distinctive
timbres and cadences,
and yet more ancient and tragic even than that.
Listen and learn: the tom sits on the garden fence
strumming his soul and letting loose
cries of infatuation
straight into the gaze of his beloved,
who then shows her gratitude
with a slash of claws across his big face;
a tattered ear and raked fur are his only reward.
But he's undaunted: off he swaggers
to his next tryst,
a new old song ready in his throat.

The Canoodling

Can I canoodle
in your canoe?
That was it, wasn't it?
Then dah dah something
canoodle with you.
I can give you oodles
of kisses and canoodles.
No, wait . . . something something something
in your canoe!
Something like that.

The Connoisseur

Tip: take a good sip of the chilled wine.
Don't swallow. Keep it steady
in the cup of your tongue,
but not for so long that it warms unduly.
Smile, be a sphinx, while the other talks and drinks.
Then, at the judicious moment, lean forward
for the possibly not unexpected kiss.
When lips touch, tip the whole lot
into the opposite mouth, as it readily opens.
Most will come back, warmer, but still
with a chill edge to it, and tastily laced
with saliva. Yum! If a drip escapes,
catch it on the tip of your tongue;
lick to mop up. Best, though, if you can niftily
slip the liquid back and forth,
losing not a drop, so the gullet can claim
its modest dividend at each swap.
Snog till dry, then sit back and wait
for the next sly opportunity.
As for the right wine:
a tip-top Sancerre, or Pouilly-Fumé,
is what I'd recommend – though, truly,
any old white would do just fine.

The Corncrake

'Won't you come out of hiding, shy bird?'
the birdcatcher sings. 'I love you, my corncrake,
my little *Crex crex*!'
The corncrake has heard, but suspects
a ruse; so she'll stay in the grass
where her eggs are, and let him pass
with his sly endearments, his importunate use
of personal pronoun. She won't step out to greet him –
no, she won't make that mistake.
She won't even reply.

The Clarinet

Lecherous liquorice stick,
with equal ease
you do sweet, you do salty,
you do blue, you do blithe,
you do blabbermouth and bigshot,
you do slow and not so slow,
you do quick and double-quick.
As soon as lips, tongue
and nimble fingers have primed you,
you're off to play
among your several registers:
from low and guttural,
mucky-edged, molasses-black,
no-apologies down and dirty,
through middle regions
of melisma and vibrato,
where extravagant soul-vistas
may tempt you to linger –
but you can't, because nobody's
allowed to live forever –
to those heights where things are apt
to move at a lick,
scampering headlong, squealy-slick,
towards a conclusion
both triumphant and sad.
Then, indefatigable
Jim Dandy, Jack the Lad,
as if you'd learned nothing,
you start up again.

The Concept

Here's my idea: I'll ransack
your wardrobe and drawers
for the naughtiest bits and pieces
I can find to put on,
while you jump into these things of mine.
Then you be me and I'll be you,
okay? Only, we're strangers,
we've never met before. So,
when you burst in, you're not exactly
expecting this gorgeous vision
in fishnet tights and feather boa,
whatever, to be lolling on your bed.
I mean, my bed. At which point –
well, it's up to you. Any wild fancy
that comes into your head.
That's the concept. Understood?
Good. Now let's get started.
Let's have some fun.

The Confusions

Marcello is betrothed to Magdalena,
who believes that he is in love with Mirabella,
her identical twin sister. Both indeed
are infatuated with Marcello,
who, however, unbeknownst to them,
has forsworn the company of women
and resolved to take monastic vows.
Fleeing the city to avoid the wrath of his father,
the Duke of Mantua, who has arranged
the match with Magdalena for purely monetary reasons,
Marcello meets on the road a young monk, Fra Martino,
who is in fact his fiancée's sister's maid, Martina,
in disguise. Martina has a plan to bring Marcello
and her mistress together by means of a magic potion
brewed in the mountains by an old witch, Morgana,
the Duke's half-sister, banished there many years before.
Meanwhile, a malcontent courtier, Malcontento,
has been plotting the abduction of Magdalena
with two henchmen, Muffo and Mosca,
instructing them to carry her off to a cave
in the mountains, by chance not far from the monastery
to which Marcello and Fra Martino are bound.
During a thunderstorm, they seek shelter in the cave,
where they find the unconscious body of Mirabella,
whom Muffo and Mosca have mistaken for her sister
and kidnapped in her place. In Act 2 . . .

The Craving

A friend of mine wanted to bed a schoolgirl:
not a particular specimen, more the general idea.
The notion entered his head one day, quite idly,
and it threatened to stay there, nagging him,
until he did something positive to appease it.
So he got in touch with a 'naughty girl'
who'd left her business card in a back-street phone booth
and, in half a jiff, he was jabbing at the bell
of a flat in Paddington, heart thumping hard,
damp-pawed and dry-throated, wondering whether
to cut and run. Too late! The door opened
and there she stood in navy gymslip and pigtails,
dangling a plaited leather switch from one hand.
In at the deep end . . . Of course, it was no good. The girl
must have been about thirty years older
than the average O-level candidate and her performance
was hopeless: less naughty, my friend said,
than plain shirty – as if she were taking particular pains
to be bad at it. To get her topless, he had to bung her
an extra ten quid. It was not what he had imagined at all
and he was glad to scamper away. What did he learn, then,
from an experience so sordid? Not much. And the itch
is still there, which he'll have to satisfy some day.

The Chop

'Oh,' she replies, off-hand,
'I gave him the chop.'
And I should be delighted,
but promptly there comes to mind
a frowning head, haggard,
shaggy-bearded and hacked
from its vital supply lines,
on a big plate, in a sop
of its own fresh blood,
presented at table to teach
a weak-willed king
a thing or two about fate.

The Crossroads

At the foredoomed crossroads, he came
face to face with the Sphinx,
who put to him her usual riddle:
'Name the creature that in the morning
walks on four legs' – et cetera;
you know the rest. He thought hard,
gave it his best shot, was wrong,
prepared to die. Then she said:
'You've no idea how lucky you are.
The next traveller along this road
will have killed his father, be about
to marry his mother, will go mad
when he finds out, will blind himself,
then wander far and wide
on a futile quest, lamenting,
before being torn to shreds by the Furies.
Be glad you've been spared
all that Freudian shemozzle.'
In the few seconds left of his life,
he pondered these words, then replied:
'I'm married already and my wife
is beyond doubt not my mother.
My father's still alive, God bless him.
I don't know why you're telling me this.
None of these horrible things was going
to happen to me.' 'Don't quibble,'
the Sphinx told him; 'it's not your place.
You're without significance, so far
as the bigger story's concerned.'

With that, she killed him,
taking care, however, to make
a neat job of it, solemnly aware
that he was to be her final victim.

The Competition

after Sappho

He must think he's in heaven,
sitting so close to you
and lapping up all
your chatter and laughter.
But it's hell for me.
In your company, my voice
dries utterly, tongue's
an unliftable weight,
fire courses through me,
eyes blear, ears roar,
I'm in a muck sweat,
boast less colour
than a wisp of straw,
and might as well be dying.

The Change

The goddess with her killer glare:
no problem there. I've seen that look myself
often enough, aimed straight at me,
and it wasn't hard to swivel it
through ninety degrees and fix it in profile.
(That dinky quiver, wrong size for the bow,
I'll adjust later.) The dogs, too, I can handle,
if I can keep the brushwork fluent:
less a pack of them than a flood, a torrent,
of muscular flanks and backs and squabbling
yelps and scent-maddened muzzles
dragging your man down. Now, he's the trouble,
which is why I've put him in the middle distance,
an arrow's flight away. He's turning into a stag.
But how do you do that, exactly?
Head first, as I've tried here, following Ovid?
Ping! – he's got antlers and a long neck,
but the rest of his body's slow on the uptake,
so he's left looking less like prey brought low
than some tipsy idiot taking a spill at a carnival?
Forget it. What I want is the change itself,
when he's neither man nor beast, or somehow both
    at once,
and you don't just see but feel the combined
horror and justice of his fate. Some way to go.
Never mind, I can be patient. It can wait.

The Clew

Sure enough, the ball of yarn she had given him,
tightly wound and slightly heavier than it looked,
did the trick. While she looped the loose end
round her middle finger, he dropped the rest
and watched it roll down what must have been
an imperceptible incline. He stooped, as if in pursuit
of a runaway toddler. At the first fork, the ball
turned left; at the next, left again. Never a second's
hesitation! It seemed to have a mind of its own;
to be, in fact, clever. Dwindling but purposeful,
it guided – beckoned him, you might say –
through passages narrower and narrower,
towards a deeper dark, a fouler stink,
where her brother, the bull-man, cowered,
snivelled and blinked: a top-heavy monster,
easily overpowered. His killer picked up the thread,
now wholly unravelled, and, too distracted to make
a proper ball, gathered it into his arms, until it led
back to the mouth of the labyrinth. There,
unwound from her finger, it was allowed to fall,
in a tangle, to the ground.

The Caress

after Pushkin

She's flashing you such smiles,
her talk's such a fountain, or firework display,
of wit and delight,
and her eyes are so needily
eating you up,
no one would guess that only last night
she used her wiles
to smuggle her little foot
all the way under the dinner table
for me to caress.

The Clatter

after Sei Shōnagon

Most annoying, the lover
who, making a dawn departure,
suddenly remembers the book,
or the keys, he has put down somewhere.
He clatters around in the dark,
muttering, less to himself than to you,
'I don't understand it';
and then, when he's found it,
the book goes into his bag
with a histrionic gesture,
or he jingles the keys
like some primitive musical instrument –
all to the detriment
of the mood of gentle regret
that you ought to be enjoying.
Instead, you can only get madder
and madder at his doltish behaviour.
Rule one: a good lover
must also be a good leaver.

The Cage

after Montaigne

A good one is rare, which is why we esteem it and value it.
If you manage it right, there's nothing in society to beat it.
We need it, and yet we habitually pooh-pooh it.
It's like a cage, where the birds outside are desperate to get
    into it,
while those locked in are just as wild to escape it.
Asked which was the better course, to embrace it or to
    eschew it,
Socrates replied: Choose either and you'll rue it.

The Capsule

It must have been love once.
That's what our operators told us:
love so perfect, we could survive,
the two of us, anything.
So we became this dwindling blip
in the firmament, set on a blind,
ever-outward course, towards
whatever destination they had in mind –
they never said; we never asked.
Instead, we let them put us on board
this tight little ship, stocked
with food, fuel, air, medication
and entertainment enough
to sustain a pair of the longest lifetimes,
then shoot us into the blue.
For a while, we were all we needed.
Such overflowing supply of the other
could scarcely run dry!
Control looked on, approvingly.
We logged our ecstatic reports.
The experiment went like a dream, like a dive
that need never arrive . . .
Precisely when, or how, we lost touch
with our faraway masters, we don't know.
Was it some technical disaster,
or part of the plan?
In the subsequent years (bottled-up
with our sour recriminations)
it has been all too easy

to cast the blame back to them,
or to and fro. There must be
some better way, I think and pray,
as our capsule, bearing its queasy
human cargo, maintains its course,
steady and lost, alongside
the shifting constellations.

The Conversation

Out of her sleep, out of a dream perhaps,
with her back turned, but plainly addressing him,
she muttered a few words: semantic scraps,
random, loose and light as blown litter,
forming a sort of sentence, or sketch of a sentence –
scarcely more than that. After a short pause,
from his own, undisturbed sleep,
he answered in a similar mutter,
just as inconsequentially and as sparsely.
The conversation – burble, burble – ended there.
If anyone else had happened to be in that room
that night, standing by the bed and leaning
close enough to overhear, think what terrific
secrets they might have learned
from verbal traffic so slight,
so empty of sense, but so full of meaning.

The Crowd

I am the crowd. I am the crowd
that throngs and thrives behind your eyes,
when they are shut. My eyes are shut too,
and that is when I am most in your head,
exercising my multiplicity:
such adroit shape-shiftings and adaptations
to your caprices and greedy needs!
Proteus, Thetis – which of the old,
fickle, fatal nymphs or demigods
can match my cunning? One moment
I am a man-eating blonde, with carmine
leer and boobs like cushions,
whom you must wrestle to subdue;
the next, a simpering waif whose gaze
you long to drown in. And there's an infinity
of more. What tricks, what stunts,
what clowning from your circus of monkeys!
What a jamboree, what a riot of sex!
And the funny thing is, no one suspects
I am in on the act. Look, here I am,
supine, naked, obedient, and my thoughts –
where, exactly? Sweetheart, are you
as safe as you think? Do you feel no disquiet?

The Cufflinks

Why, when asked what she had given him
for his birthday, did he reply,
not 'Cufflinks' – actually, a unique pair,
Art Deco, in silver, lapis and vermeil,
whose market value he didn't care
even to guess at – but 'Handcuffs'?

The Chaos

A beat of a butterfly's wing was all it took,
a next-to-nothing thing, a blink, a flicker,
registered not so much in the eye, or the brain,
as in the blood, or a cell of the blood,
a micro-event, but big enough
to be followed by another, bigger,
so that, by a series of trips, or triggers,
each one unstoppable, each an acceleration
and magnification beyond all proportion –
first words of formal greeting, wry
recognition of what must be left unsaid,
a second meeting, touches, kisses, bed,
and so on – the weather on the opposite side
of the world was changed, and a marriage
hurled to perdition by a force in the sky
equivalent to apocalypse.

The Cheat

First time, it was scary, sickening,
but also a high, a thrill.
Departure from the marriage script
meant recourse to a skill
for reckless improvisation
last used in his early twenties.
To his exhilaration, he found
he could look his wife full in the eye
while stepping out on to the tightrope
of a lie with no end in sight
and a measureless drop beneath it.
The fling, being trivial and short,
passed undetected, as did the next two,
with their addictive blend
of fun and fear. In subsequent
escapades – ever less meaningful,
ever less meant – the fear, to a large extent,
became the fun, a toxic
and irresistible rush, and the women concerned
increasingly abstract excuses for it.
When his wife learned of the last one,
the bathos was too much to bear.
He had expected something ecstatic,
a sublime death under the pounce
and sweetly anaesthetising breath
of a big cat, but instead got
a note on the kitchen table,
months of bickering with literal-minded
lawyers, and a poky flat on the outskirts of town.
How could he have been so blinded?

The Cupboard

My lover keeps me in a cupboard.
I've no complaints. There's room enough,
on my own, high, private shelf,
to stretch myself out for the hours, the days,
the weeks of muffled waiting
that he requires of me. He puts
a finger to his lips, raises his eyebrows
archly and, without a further word,
shuts the door. Hearing it click,
I make a pillow of my hands, adjust
my hip to the unyielding board,
prepare to sleep. Sometimes I wake
to voices on the other side –
of business colleagues, friends,
even his wife – or that most plaintive cry
of a phone in an empty office.
But such interludes soon pass, and I
return to my pharaonic rest.
Outside of sleep, I like the small hours best,
when it can be hard to tell the night city's
unceasing traffic from the rumble of blood
in my own head. Then, in the stale dark,
I know I have the patience and the power
to win this long game. The world and my waiting
are one and the same.

The Climax

Not until the last bars of the symphony
did the critic get the point. It was the point
of a knife. For twenty minutes, he had been preparing
the usual put-downs, ironies and mockeries.
(The composer knew them well.)
Then something began to swell
in the orchestra. Little touches at first:
muted trombones, increasingly urgent,
throaty clarinets, harmonic frissons from the upper strings.
The composer, at the rostrum, coaxed the musicians on,
with gestures like caresses, the sound inexorably building.
By the time the timpani started to pound
against brass gasps and woodwind yelps –
a miracle of orchestration – the critic was in no doubt:
the bastard had been screwing his wife!

The Cyclists

The cyclists took the corner
in italics. An entire paragraph.
We drew in and let them hurtle by.
Lean, fixed on speed,
they paid no attention to us.
They were a flashed warrant,
an illegible screed
of backs uniformly cursive
and curlicued handlebars.
Or a thigh-powered,
air-slicing machine
for clearing the roads of France.
Or the corps de ballet
in its celebrated showstopper,
Get Out of Our Way!
Or – in helmets, goggles
and gaudy lycra –
a new species of insect,
related to the grasshopper
and, through some fluke of evolution,
blessed with wheels.
Windows down, we felt their breeze.
But they paid no attention to us.
Sly, weekend lovers, we were less
than a footnote. The text
had only itself to please.

The Card

I had just popped into one of those public conveniences
from which you can also make phone calls, intending
to make a phone call, when my eye was distracted
by your card: your madly complicated
leathers, your whip raised in a dainty
and ineffectual grip, your badly acted
sneer of cold command – every detail designed
to break, if not the heart or spirit,
the mind. My hand edged, first, towards it,
then away. Forgetting my call,
I left that astringently reeking place
at double the pace, wondering: would I dare
confront such innocence in the flesh?
And if so, how much might I have to pay?

The Crime

Evidence of haste and shame, in the way
this glossy lads' mag has been ripped
not quite in two, thrown down in the road –
from a passing car? by a late-night walker? –
and left to die. A forensic March wind
pokes at the pages, identifying
here a lone nipple, there a length of thigh.

The Curse

after Catullus

May she not just live but flourish
in the company of her seducers,
holding all three hundred at once
in a comprehensive embrace,
showing true love to none but doing
steady damage to their pelvises,
and may she never cast a glance
back to my love, as it once was,
which, thanks to her, has died
like a flower in some remote meadow,
clipped by the passing plough.

The Cavalry

after Apollinaire

By God, war's fun! We sing
and loaf about. I've put
quite a shine on this ring.
The wind's one with your sighs.
Hey, that's Boots and Saddles! Goodbye!
And he galloped off round the bend,
which is where he met his end.
She laughed out loud at fate's
capacity to surprise.

The Cab

Those last years he spent
assembling and curating
his Museum of Erotic Memories.
It filled most of his house in Notting Hill,
which came more and more
to resemble a junk shop:
every wall and shelf,
and much of the floor-space,
cluttered with exhibits –
some saved by himself,
some bought back from, or lent by,
indulgent ex-lovers,
some less honestly acquired –
all to be admired
in private reverie.
By the time he died, he had amassed
seventy per cent of his love letters
and numerous notes and scrawls
of a more spontaneous nature –
'Darling, I'll miss you!'
being a recurrent phrase –
on calling cards, menus, LP sleeves,
even scraps of tissue.
Period lipstick cylinders and perfume bottles
were another speciality, as well as items
of recherché underwear,
somehow retrieved
from the darkness and disorder
of the long past.

Then there were beds, a motley procession.
Pride of place, however,
went to the black London cab –
the actual one, whose licence number
he had taken care to remember –
where the whole, sweet,
headlong business had begun,
with some hot kisses and hurried fumbling,
just out of sight of the shoppers
in Kensington Church Street,
while the meter kept ticking
and the driver sat impassive
as the priest at confession.

The Copy

Six months or so after his wife died,
he was looking for a copy. Why not?
Given the millions of thirty-something women
out there in the world, it wasn't such a long shot.
But how to begin? How to advertise his requirements?
He put a notice in the local paper: age, height,
colour of hair and eyes. Neither applicant was remotely
    right.
So he tried new pubs and clubs, enrolled for evening
    classes,
took seaside holidays, prowled the streets
of the capital. There, one night, he was beaten up
when he asked a girl in a doorway if she wouldn't mind
angling her face a little towards the lamplight.
Not quite unconscious, he was dismayed
by the obvious wrongness of her laughter.

The Circumstances

after Cavafy

They were both distraught
at having to part.
Neither wanted to,
but circumstances forced them.
A job had come up,
obliging one of them
to move far away –
somewhere in America.
To be frank, their love
was not what it had once been:
mutual attraction
had grown less intense,
and the power of love itself
much less intense.
Still, they were reluctant
to be separated.
Circumstance, though,
or possibly Fate –
with an artist's touch –
was parting them now,
before affection faded,
before time could change them,
so that each for the other
would stay as he had always been:
a handsome young man
in his early twenties.

The Confessions

That time in the darkening park:
the girl, with her back to a tree,
close enough for the edge of something
sourish on her breath – milk
from a not so recent cup of tea? –
to be part of the warmth of her, part
of the unspoken invitation,
and yet he failed to cross
that last, short distance. Or,
called to a flat in a neighbourhood
of tenebrous mansion blocks
and padlocked gardens, where he found
his hostess still in her bath,
and so stood out in the passage, feeding
small talk through the gap
of the door, knowing he might,
in another life, have stepped
straight into the steam and fragrance. Or
that night of the dance,
when a new acquaintance
took him to bed, and it was no dream,
but, instead of exploring
the curious twists and turns
of her lips or fondling her nice,
trim bum, he lay there inert,
overcome by some inarticulate scruple. Or . . .

The Crotchet

The trick you had on occasion,
mid-embrace,
of using the tip of my nose
to push your slipped spectacles
back up the slope of your nose
to their proper place:
I could never on the spot
decide whether I should be
amused or irritated;
and – you know what? –
only now do I see
how neither response was right,
and that I was simply an uptight,
slow-on-the-uptake
beneficiary of your grace.

The Crow

No, he's not. He's just a crow,
doing his crow thing:
black garb, harsh cry,
stiff strut. Yet it's his lot
to appear less bird
than myth. Descending
on the ridge of a roof,
he becomes his own
heraldic logo, cloaked
silhouette, till he tires of that
and releases himself
with a lavish, all-elbows show
of up-floundering aerodynamics.
You've heard a sky
full of his ego-strife
and bullying panics.
Courtship for him
is arranging his feathers
askew and doing a truculent
war-jig in front of the object
of his desire; and yet they say
he mates for life. Even so,
you mustn't forget:
he's just a crow.

The Centaur

From the outset, tongues clacked
in a chorus of gossip and censure.
What could she be thinking of,
the king's daughter, flaunting her hot
and reckless fling with that Centaur?
It wasn't just a question of rank
or decorum; there were the biological
what-d'you-call-'ems to consider:
her barely nubile sylphlikeness
against his hundredweights of panting,
steaming horseflesh – no! It wasn't right!
The whole thing was an affront to nature
and could only, the chorus agreed,
end messily. Which it did. Yet for a while
they were the happiest couple in all Thessaly.

The Credits

My thanks to the editors of the following publications in which some of these poems, or versions of them, first appeared: *Areté*, *The Art of Wiring* (Ondt & Gracehoper), *Birdbook 3* (Sidekick Books), *Drift*, *Jubilee Lines* (Faber and Faber), *London Magazine*, *Magma*, *Metamorphosis: Poems Inspired by Titian* (National Gallery), *New Walk*, *New Writing Dundee*, *New Yorker*, *The Palm Beach Effect: Reflections on Michael Hofmann* (CB editions), *A Poetic Primer for Love and Seduction: Naso Was My Tutor* (Emma Press), *Poetry London*, *Poetry Review*, *Prague Review*, *Red: A Waterstones Anthology*, *Southwords*, *Spectator*, *Under Travelling Skies* (Kingston Press), *Warwick Review*, *Wenlock Poetry Festival Anthology 2012* and *Yellow Nib*.

I could not have made my versions of certain foreign-language poems (and one prose passage) without the intermediary translations of Dafydd Johnston, editor of *Canu Maswedd yr Oesoedd Canol/Medieval Welsh Erotic Poetry* (Seren), George Kay, editor of *The Penguin Book of Italian Verse*, Ivan Morris, translator of *The Pillow Book of Sei Shōnagon* (Penguin Classics), Dmitri Obolensky, editor of *The Penguin Book of Russian Verse*, and Edward Snow, translator of Rilke's *New Poems [1907]* (North Point Press); and I am duly grateful to them.

Thanks also to Simon Barraclough, Isobel Dixon, Katy Evans-Bush, Luke Heeley, Matthew Hollis, Kirsten Irving, Ann Pasternak Slater, Liane Strauss and Róisín Tierney for advice on, and improvements to, some of this work.